Kansas

BY EMMA HUDDLESTON

CONTENT CONSULTANT
Kristen Epps, PhD
Associate Professor of History
Managing Editor of *Kansas History*
Kansas State University

Core Library

An Imprint of Abdo Publishing
abdobooks.com

abdobooks.com

Printed in the United States of America, North Mankato, Minnesota.
052022
092022

THIS BOOK CONTAINS
RECYCLED MATERIALS

Cover Photos: Shutterstock Images, map and illustrations, cattle
Interior Photos: Tommy Brison/Shutterstock Images, 4–5; Red Line Editorial, 9 (Kansas), 9 (USA); Orlin Wagner/AP Images, 10–11; K. Swinicki/Shutterstock Images, 12, 34; Mark Reinstein/Corbis/ Getty Images, 15; iStockphoto, 17 (flag); Shutterstock Images, 17 (bison); David Spates/Shutterstock Images, 17 (meadowlark); Sari ONeal/Shutterstock Images, 17 (sunflower); K. E. Photography/ Shutterstock Images, 17 (tree); Gino Santa Maria/Shutterstock Images, 20, 43; Alex Potemkin/ iStockphoto, 22–23; Michael Vorobiev/Shutterstock Images, 26; Ricardo Reitmeyer/Shutterstock Images, 28, 45; Mary Vanier/Shutterstock Images, 30–31; Sean Pavone/Shutterstock Images, 36–37

Editor: Marie Pearson
Series Designer: Joshua Olson

Library of Congress Control Number: 2021951416

Publisher's Cataloging-in-Publication Data

Names: Huddleston, Emma, author.
Title: Kansas / by Emma Huddleston
Description: Minneapolis, Minnesota : Abdo Publishing, 2023 | Series: Core library of US states | Includes online resources and index.
Identifiers: ISBN 9781532197574 (lib. bdg.) | ISBN 9781098270339 (ebook)
Subjects: LCSH: U.S. states--Juvenile literature. | Midwest States--Juvenile literature. | Kansas-- History--Juvenile literature. | Physical geography--United States--Juvenile literature.
Classification: DDC 978.1--dc23

Population demographics broken down by race and ethnicity come from the 2019 census estimate. Population totals come from the 2020 census.

CONTENTS

THE SUNFLOWER STATE

Sunshine warms a sunflower's yellow petals. Big green leaves grow out from its thick stem. People walk along trails through fields of sunflowers at a farm in Clearwater, Kansas. Many people have to look up to see the flowers. Sunflowers grow up to 12 feet (3.7 m) tall. A family stops to take a photo. Kansas is nicknamed the Sunflower State because of the sunflowers that commonly grow there.

Sunflowers are grown for their edible seeds and the oil that can be made from them.

OLDEST CITY

Leavenworth is the oldest city in Kansas. It offers historic sites such as an old military fort. Fort Leavenworth first opened in 1827. The US military still uses it today, making it one of the oldest continuously used forts in the country. There are five active US prisons in and around Leavenworth. One former military prison began operating in 1875. It stopped housing prisoners in 2002. Now it's a museum for people to learn about military history.

GET TO KNOW KANSAS

Kansas is part of the Midwest. This region of the United States is known for farming. Kansas is bordered by Nebraska to the north and Oklahoma to the south. Its western border touches Colorado. The eastern border touches Missouri.

Kansas is part of the Great Plains. This group of states has expanses of prairie land and farmland. Crops such as wheat, oats, and corn grow here. Today 90 percent of Kansas's land is used for agriculture.

Most of Kansas's large cities are located in the eastern part of the state. Wichita is the largest city.

HISTORY OF KANSAS

People have lived in Kansas for at least 10,000 years. Eventually American Indian nations formed, including the Kanza, Wahzhazhe (Osage), Pawnee, and Wichita. The state of Kansas is named after the Kanza people. *Kanza* translates to "people of the south wind." Altogether they became known to European settlers as Plains Indians because they lived in the Great Plains. These nations all spoke different languages. The languages of some nations were more similar

Today some Kanza people in Kansas celebrate their culture through dance.

Bison were an important source of food and materials for some American Indian peoples in Kansas.

than others. Today most people of these nations speak English. Some also speak their traditional languages.

Early Plains Indians were hunters and gatherers. They lived in small family groups. By 850 CE, some lived in larger villages and farmed. The Kanza and Wahzhazhe settled near the Missouri River. They grew corn, beans,

KANSAS
QUICK FACTS

There is a lot that sets Kansas apart from other states. Why do you think the state symbols below are important for Kansas?

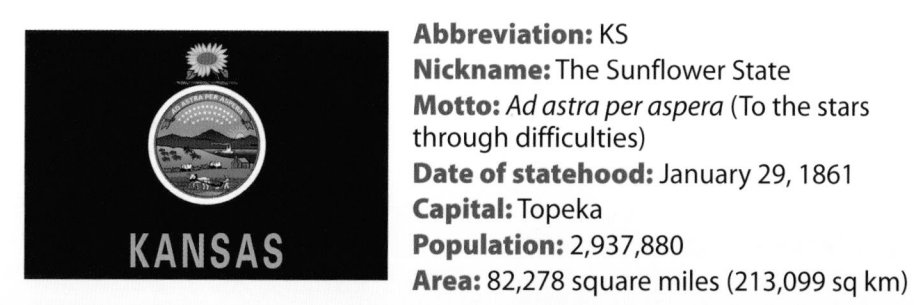

Abbreviation: KS
Nickname: The Sunflower State
Motto: *Ad astra per aspera* (To the stars through difficulties)
Date of statehood: January 29, 1861
Capital: Topeka
Population: 2,937,880
Area: 82,278 square miles (213,099 sq km)

STATE SYMBOLS

State animal
American buffalo (bison)

State flower
Wild native sunflower

State bird
Western meadowlark

State tree
Cottonwood tree

DUST BOWL

In the 1930s the Dust Bowl hit Kansas. Leading up to that time, many of Kansas's grasslands had been replaced by crop fields. Then a severe drought hit. Crops died, and the strong winds of the open plains beat at the soil. The soil dried out, and the wind whipped it up into massive dust storms. The dust blew into buildings through cracks. Outside it was difficult or impossible to breathe or see. Some people left. Others stayed and changed their farming methods to prevent another Dust Bowl. They planted grasses in some of the fields to protect the soil. They planted trees to break the wind.

Act of 1862 urged people to move. With this act, the US government promised people land in exchange for moving to and working in the west. More American Indian peoples were forced onto reservations as a result.

Like other Americans, Kansans also experienced challenges during World War I (1914–1918), the Great Depression (1929–1930s), and World War II (1939–1945). Throughout this time, Black people in Kansas and across

the nation continued to face discrimination. Often Black schools had fewer resources than white schools. This led to the 1954 court case *Brown v. Board of Education of Topeka.* The US Supreme Court ruled segregation of schools unfair and made it illegal.

GOVERNMENT AND MODERN LIFE

Today Kansas's government is made up of three branches. Each branch has different responsibilities.

PERSPECTIVES

AMELIA EARHART

The famous pilot Amelia Earhart was born in Kansas in 1897. She became the first woman to fly nonstop across the Atlantic Ocean in 1928. Her adventurous spirit led the way for female pilots across the country. But her death is an unsolved mystery. She began a flight around the globe in 1937. She and her plane were lost over the South Pacific Ocean and never found. A present-day family member of Earhart's is named after the famous pilot. She hopes people remember Earhart as a role model. She said, "[Earhart] left this idea that no matter what your goal is, you just have to set your mind to it and get it done."

Topeka is home to the state's capitol building.

The legislative branch makes laws. It is formed from two groups. The state Senate has 40 members, and the state House has 125 representatives. The executive branch signs laws into action. It is led by the governor. The judicial branch is the court system.

American Indians have their own governments. There are four federally recognized nations in the state today. They are the Iowa Nation of Kansas and Nebraska, Prairie Band Potawatomi Nation, Sac and Fox Nation of Missouri, and Kickapoo Tribe in Kansas. These nations can receive government funding. American Indian families from many nations call Kansas home.

STRAIGHT TO THE
SOURCE

The *Brown v. Board of Education of Topeka* court case was the start of desegregation around the country. US representative Robert Scott of Virginia spoke about the case's legacy in 2019. He said:

> *The Court's historic ruling was not the end of school segregation, it was the beginning of a long and difficult struggle to unwind centuries of systemic inequality that have influenced every aspect of American life. Today's inequity in education, housing, economic opportunity, criminal justice, and other policy areas are the legacy of our history. . . . The federal government contributed to racial segregation and inequality, so the federal government must be part of the solution.*
>
> Source: Joe Davidson. "*Brown v. Board of Education*: After 65 Years, Still Seeking to Make a Promise a Reality." *Washington Post*, 3 May 2019, washingtonpost.com. Accessed 12 Jan. 2021.

BACK IT UP

Scott is using evidence to support a point. Write a paragraph describing the point Scott is making. Then write down two or three pieces of evidence he uses to make the point.

This makes the Ozark Plateau a rich mining location. Hardwood trees such as oaks and hickories grow in this region.

PLANTS AND ANIMALS

Prairie grasses and wildflowers grow throughout the state. Prairie grasses have deep roots. This helps them store water and stay in place during strong winds. The grasses protect soil so it doesn't blow away. The state grass is the little bluestem. It thrives in the Flint Hills. This area includes some of the last unplowed stretches of true prairie in the country. Only 4 percent of the

PRAIRIE CHICKENS

Western Kansas is home to the largest prairie chicken population in the United States. This animal is also known as a grouse. There are several species. The greater sage grouse grows up to 2 feet (0.6 m) tall. The lesser prairie chicken is smaller. It has brown-and-white striped feathers. Both species are threatened by human activity. Buildings and oil and gas businesses are taking away prairie chicken habitat.

People can enjoy views of the tallgrass prairie at Tallgrass Prairie National Preserve.

original tallgrass prairie remains in the United States today. Some of it is protected in the Flint Hills.

The state bird, the western meadowlark, prefers grassland habitat. Bison graze on prairie grasses. Bison nearly disappeared from Kansas in the late 1800s due to overhunting. Now they are raised on ranches and farms throughout the state. Large herds can also be seen in preserves. The grasslands of Kansas are important habitats for prairie animals. They also provide land for ranches and farms throughout the state. The geography and climate of Kansas influence the livelihoods of many Kansans.

STRAIGHT TO THE
SOURCE

Kansas is an important site for fossil research. Rex Buchanan is the former director of the Kansas Geological Survey. Buchanan said:

> *Sometimes I think Kansans don't appreciate those fossils as much as they should.*
>
> *A few years ago, I led a field trip that included a stop at the Sternberg Museum in Hays. The Sternberg houses lots of jaw-dropping fossils. . . . But the people on the trip . . . seemed less than impressed. When I asked why, their responses harkened back to our good old Kansas inferiority complex. If these fossils are here in Kansas, folks wondered, how good could they be? The thing is, fossils from Kansas . . . are displayed in big-time museums all over the world.*

Source: Rex Buchanan. "Kansas: Land of Famous Fossils." *Kansas Public Radio*, 17 July 2018, kansaspublicradio.org. Accessed 19 Jan. 2021.

WHAT'S THE BIG IDEA?

Take a close look at this passage. What is the main connection being made between Kansas and the fossils discovered there? How does Buchanan think people should react when viewing these fossils?

RESOURCES AND ECONOMY

The history of Kansas's economy focuses on mining and agriculture. In the 1870s lead and zinc were discovered in southeastern Kansas. People started mining in the Ozark Plateau region. For the next 100 years, Kansas was a top US producer of those materials. Lead is used to make batteries. Zinc is used in some medicines. It is also used to coat iron and steel to prevent rusting.

Some Kansas ranches raise beef cattle.

HOW SEDIMENTARY ROCKS FORM

Most rocks in Kansas are sedimentary. Sedimentary rocks form near Earth's surface. Layers of organic material such as dead plants and animals pile up. Over millions of years, the material is pressed together. It hardens into rock. Sedimentary rock can also have layers of inorganic materials such as bits of sand and clay. Smaller pieces of rock or other materials press together. They likewise harden into rock. The sedimentary rock in Kansas is made of many different minerals. That is why Kansas is ideal for mining.

Kansas was one of the top three states in cattle production in the 1890s. Agriculture continues to be important today. The state's fertile soil and open land make it ideal for farming and raising livestock. Kansas is a top producer of wheat and sorghum grains. Its other major products are wild hay, beef, and hogs.

Kansas is a top state for mining minerals such as gypsum. The Gypsum Hills are located in south-central Kansas. Gypsum is used to make cement. Rocks in

western Kansas provide huge amounts of chalk. Central Kansas has a massive rock salt supply underground. Rock salt is used to make table salt. By 1970 the lead and zinc mines had closed in part due to concerns about their effects on the environment. But other building materials continue to be mined in Kansas. These include stone, clay, sand, and gravel.

Natural resources and agricultural materials benefit the manufacturing industry. Manufacturing is another major part of Kansas's economy. Materials produced in the state are easily

Wind energy generation is growing in Kansas.

available to factories. Wichita is a manufacturing center. Its factories make camping gear, heating and air conditioning units, and snowmobiles. They also make military aircraft equipment. Other factories throughout the state make baby food and pet food. Products such as mobile homes, greeting cards, tires, and paint are also made in Kansas.

Kansas produces energy from several sources. Oil and gas are found throughout the state, especially in

the central and southern areas. Coal used to be mined in Kansas. But those mines had closed by 2016 due in part to dropping demand.

In recent years, Kansas has focused on growing its wind energy production. The state's open fields give room for wind turbines. In 2019 Kansas generated more than 40 percent of its electricity from wind.

FURTHER EVIDENCE

Chapter Four talks about agriculture as one major part of Kansas's economy. Identify one of the chapter's main points. What evidence does the author provide to support this point? The website at the link below also discusses agriculture in Kansas. Find a quote on this website that supports the main point you identified. Does the quote support an existing piece of evidence in the chapter? Or does it offer a new piece of evidence?

KANSAS AGRICULTURE
abdocorelibrary.com/kansas

El Cuartelejo is the northernmost pueblo ruin in the United States. A pueblo is an American Indian town of flat-roofed stone or adobe houses. In addition, 28 state parks dot Kansas. People enjoy camping and hiking. They can fish, hunt, or ride horses. From the tallgrass prairie and the Ozark Plateau to city and small-town life, Kansas is full of unique people and places.

EXPLORE ONLINE

Chapter Five discusses famous people who lived in Kansas, including James Naismith. The website below explores Naismith's journey inventing basketball. What information does the website give about basketball history? How is the information from the website the same as the information in Chapter Five? What new information did you learn from the website?

JAMES NAISMITH
abdocorelibrary.com/kansas

IMPORTANT DATES

10,000 years ago
Plains Indians live in the Kansas region. Many are hunters and gatherers.

1541
Spanish explorers come north from Mexico looking for gold.

1830s–1840s
Nearly 30 American Indian nations in eastern states move to Kansas after the US government forces them off their lands.

1854–1861
Kansas Territory faces violence over slavery's expansion during Bleeding Kansas.

1861
Kansas becomes the thirty-fourth US state on January 29. The American Civil War begins.

1930s
The Dust Bowl hits Kansas.

1954
In *Brown v. Board of Education of Topeka*, the US Supreme Court rules that segregation in schools is unconstitutional.

2019
Kansas gets more than 40 percent of its electricity from wind farms.

STOP AND THINK

Take a Stand

Kansas gets electricity from coal and wind. Coal mining has been important for hundreds of years. Wind is a renewable resource. Do you think one type of energy is better than the other? Or do you think both have benefits and drawbacks? Why?

Surprise Me

Chapter Five discusses people and places in Kansas. After reading this book, what two or three facts about Kansas did you find most surprising? Write a few sentences about each fact. Why did you find each fact surprising?

Dig Deeper

After reading this book, what questions do you still have about the history of Kansas? With an adult's help, find a few reliable sources that can help you answer your questions. Write a paragraph about what you learned.

Tell the Tale

Chapter Two of this book describes the Dust Bowl. Imagine you are experiencing one of the dust storms. Write 200 words about what it is like. What do you see and feel?

GLOSSARY

abolish
to officially end something

discrimination
when people treat others
differently based on certain
factors such as appearance

elevation
how high up something is

fertile
rich in nutrients for
growing plants

fossil
the preserved remains
of something that lived
long ago

Indigenous
relating to the earliest known
residents of an area

mineral
a nonliving substance found
naturally on Earth

organic
a type of substance that was
once living

plateau
high, flat land

reservation
an area of land set aside for
American Indians

segregation
the separation of groups of
people based on race, class,
or ethnicity

ONLINE RESOURCES

To learn more about Kansas, visit our free resource websites below.

Visit **abdocorelibrary.com** or scan this QR code for free Common Core resources for teachers and students, including vetted activities, multimedia, and booklinks, for deeper subject comprehension.

Visit **abdobooklinks.com** or scan this QR code for free additional online weblinks for further learning. These links are routinely monitored and updated to provide the most current information available.

LEARN MORE

Avise, Jonathan. *Sporting Kansas City.* Abdo, 2022.

Rubin, Susan Goldman. *Brown v. Board of Education: A Fight for Simple Justice.* Holiday House, 2016.

INDEX

About the Author

Emma Huddleston lives in Minnesota with her husband. She enjoys writing children's books and reading mystery novels. She has been to 18 US states and hopes to visit many more!